The Naked Man

poems by

Christine Irving

*Dedicated to all women everywhere
who fall prey to the charms of Naked Men*

~

Foreword

The Naked Man represents un-awakened human nature. He is *First Man* setting out on the journey of a lifetime to discover all the parts of his nature and integrate them into one wide-awake conscious being. He is happy in his naiveté but everything he encounters on his journey will conspire to destroy his innocence. Sadly, the harder he tries to hold on to it, the more tarnished and false it will become.

The Naked Man has many names and a thousand folk tales to his credit. He is Fool, Simpleton, Numskull, Dummling, Youngest Son, Third Brother, etc. In Tarot, the Fool is the one card in the deck that has no number. No number represents emptiness – though the Fool may be cunning he is empty of wisdom. The Cards of the Major Arcana, laid out in three rows of seven are said to represent the Fool's (humanity's) journey through life. Each card represents an archetypal quality common to all humans. The Fool must pass through each, exploring each quality and making it his/hers. At that time he/she once again becomes the Fool. Now his/her innocence results from being wise rather than foolish. Emptiness becomes an abundance of potential rather than a lack of resources.

Sometimes people get stuck in one archetype by mistaking a part of the puzzle for the whole picture. The Naked Man in my poems is stuck at the beginning of his journey. He teeters on the edge of the abyss unwilling to make the leap of faith which will send him tumbling out of control through all the parts of himself he most fears. He clings to the aspects of the Fool which he perceives as valuable, i.e. spontaneity, truth telling, free will, insouciance, intuitive wisdom. However, all archetypes have two sides to their character. The Naked Man fails to notice that he also embodies the flip side of the Fool's qualities. In this guise he is dismissive of the wisdom of others, uses "honesty" as a critical tool, and manipulates truth for his own ends. The Fool's lack of emotional sophistication leaves him curiously un-empathetic, though this same detachment also allows for random acts of great generosity.

He's an enchanting creature with all the appeal of the young ones of any species. But beguiling as he may be, he is not yet able to engage in emotional intimacy. Naked Men hold great charm and are immanently lovable. It makes them dangerous. If you are entangled with such a one, be prepared for a broken heart.

-Christine Irving

Table of Contents

Journey's End

The Naked Man
begins to journey
by leaving home and tumbling
into an abyss.

Free fall becomes him—
long limbs cart wheeling through air
while wife, children, house
"the full catastrophe"
sail upwards into the blue.

He's fool, simpleton
dummkopf, hobo
youngest brother;
underrated
misunderstood....

He'll suffer
strange encounters
pratfalls, stumbles.

Somewhere the Devil waits.

There are worse things than a rabbit hole.
He'll have to lose himself
to save his soul.

~

After the Night Before

The naked man, bamboozled
by rice wine and poetry
caroms through the forest
waving his pecker at the moon
searching out the oak he likes
to water by moonlight.

~

IT

The Naked Man is so good looking
when he walks in the café door
all our panties dampen.

He's got a pheromone machine inside him
churning out sex appeal.

For that, we forgive him many sins.

~

2:22 A.M.

Outside my window
the Naked Man
waters the oaks.
His moan shakes the sky
stars splash against his chest like tears.

I want to greet him
like a goddess gliding on moonlight
climb him as if he were tree
lock legs around him, teetering
on the edge of ecstasy
until his bellow tips us over.

But a chorus of frogs
(Hecate's dear familiars)
croak prophesy and counsel. Once
their words were Greek to me.
Tonight, I distinguish every warning
each syllable of sage advice.

They sing the man—
laughter, lust, tears, pain
love, despair, confusion
anger, anxiety, regret....

They sing rites of passage
harmonic progression and retreat.

Who am I to turn initiation into tragedy?

The gods
may have their way with him —
for now.

~

Year of the Tyger

The Naked Man
perfumes his armpits
with patchouli;
throws incense
on a bonfire at midnight,
leaps across flame
plunging in and out
of aromatic smoke
agile as a ping-pong ball.

Fragrance spirals
up like prayer
greets galaxies, mingles
with the Lesser
Magallenic Cloud.

Deep in the wood
a tiger coughs.
Moonlight silvers tawny pelt
burnishes dark stripes
to ebony.

She hunts, stalking
his heightened heartbeat
scenting blood
beneath that fragrant cloud.

Fire gives her pause.
Golden eyes reflect bright flame.

The man, drunk on solitude and stars
woos animal with words.
"Tyger!" he calls, praising
her bright eye. "Come
make love to me."

~

Gratitude

Eros snuck in and kissed
me on the cheek last night
tweaked my nipples
stirred my honey pot.

He's a chip off the old marble block—
Mama's boy, schooled
in Earth magic;
spells of sensuality,
entrancements of desire.

Tomorrow I'll visit Aphrodite,
sweep the temple floor
light incense, feed her serpents
milk and mice, heap pomegranates
figs and pears upon her altar.

I know who sent him on this errand.

~

Wagging the Dog

Two dawns ago a dog
leapt out of my poem
rushed headfirst down the lane
found you
peeing on an oak tree
and goosed you
with his cold wet nose.

You yelped.

I smiled to see you there
(standing in the all together)
envied the dog's
determined assault—
his lapping tongue
his fearless intimacy.

If I
write myself
into this story
naked, unafraid and brash
what becomes of the dog?

~

Encounter

The Goddess, on meeting
the blue Mad Bad Dog
(kissing cousin to Coyote)
contemplates her direction:
approach...retreat...flight?

He stands his ground
offering to play stick
letting her
make the first
bold move....

~

Desperate

Sometimes the Naked Man
runs like a mad dog
through bad blue midnights
trailing moon shadows and tears.

~

Blue Moon

The mad bad dog
bays at the moon till his balls
turn blue.

Strangely attracted, she rises
twice to meet him;
full and round
blushing aqua
as she comes.

~

The Naked Man Creates a Disturbance

The Naked Man
has taken to wearing
Harlequin tights
and size twelve
dancing slippers
to walk the power lines
strung across Zion Street
in front of SPD grocery store
where banners hang advertising
craft fairs and Christmas pageants.
He carries a sign
that says, "Stop the War."
I hope he's got
insurance.

~

Common Ground

The Naked Man and I
have something in common—
when they (whoever they are)
handed out the script
(the one that tells you how
to act like other people)
we hid behind a door somewhere
in the hapless way of children
who have no hope
of never being found.

~

Intimacy

The Naked Man and I have made a pact.
He begged intimacy and I, touched
by being offered freely a prize
too often hard won and illusive,
fell into agreement.

Now I puzzle over what we meant—
agreeing without definition on something indeterminate,
quicksilver in its movement: eelish, slippery, vague
yet permanent and poignant—fixed point
of longing and desire.

~

You Said

I heard you say
you'd figured it already
leapfrog mind so facile—
astoundingly like mine
in instant comprehension.

Thus, I dare extrapolate
(knowing how for me
emotion lags, fails to surface
in the moment, blindsiding
hours later...)

that, jet lag notwithstanding
time, place, emotion, archetype & memory
will someday synchronize their watches
and come together in an orgasm
of comprehension, to present
a reckoning, you can neither
figure out nor flee.

~

Shape Shifter

Last night the Naked Man
stumbled into my dreams
tumbling across my threshold
like a Fool feigning innocence.

He came as shape shifter
flickering swiftly from form to form
fish, eel, dog, monkey, shaman.

The moon rose between us mirror bright.
Seen through her light, he seemed
but shadow; postulated, abstract, floating
across a silver screen.

I dreamed I stepped forward
breaching white fire. It burned
but did not scorch, flamed
but did not consume.

The man stood bare before me
truly naked at last...

silence replaced words
hardened into flesh; his kiss
melted like butterscotch
into my whole mouth.

~

Relentless

Clear-eyed, open-faced
smiling a rascal smile
he turns, contradicts
deflects, denies.

Relentless obfuscation
keeps him skating
on the literal;
dodging and ducking
so swiftly
thin ice cannot crack
and send him plumbing
unknown depths
to risk the bends
and suffer
a sea change.

~

Tipping Point

He wants to make love to me, in the street to stop the war.
For a moment, I suspend disbelief: imagine
unbuttoning his shirt, dropping jeans to the pavement.
Somewhere the thousandth monkey
swings through jungle canopy
a butterfly flaps her wings—tsunamis hit Japan; I
can almost feel asphalt bite my cold bare butt
hear honking horns and sirens—"Okay," I say
but he grabs my hand and pulls us from the crosswalk.
"Would you do it, to stop the war?" he asks.
"Sure, but I don't believe it will."
"Thank God," he says, shivering in the cold wind.

I could fall in love with *that* naked honesty but he
rewraps himself in glamour as if it were a warm jacket
recommences falling, whirling,
twirling through archetypal space....

He knows not what he conjures with
how wild I really am, what depths of courage
I may call upon at will.... Eros will never
match Kali's inexhaustible
tolerance for chaos. She moves within me
like magma, earthquake, floodtide and tornado.
Next time he throws a challenge down,
he'd best be ready.

~

This Minuet

The Naked Man and I
begin another round.

This lengthy minuet;
advance, retreat
curtsy, bow
change partner
and reform
has already
lasted too long.

I'd rather tango.

~

Idyll Worship

The Naked Man
found a plastic blow up doll
stuffed behind the dumpster.

He's trimmed his favorite spots
with emerald moss
and artful scarlet
raspberries; yesterday
he added a tiara.

He's creating a goddess
beautiful as a woman
whose mirror eyes will never cry
whose sweet deep throat
remains quiescent.

~

Cheap Thrills

The Naked Man stands on a soap box
expounding at length, drawing pictures in the sand.
He flings eloquent hands in graphic gesture,
hawking the latest advancements in marital aids—
sabled ankle cuffs, purple plumes (guaranteed to fluff)
exotic DVD's and edible oils.

I watch his mouth shape sounds
tiny muscles, delicate precise
each movement echoed deep inside
my own interior.

Some women find men's forearms
erotically appealing,
I prefer their upper lips.

He shapes each word
with delicate configurations
slight as kisses brushed across a thigh.

I pray he spins this elocution
long enough that I might come
secretly sweetly, of my own volition—
the only aid his mobile mouth
and my imagination.

~

hung over

stubble faced, dirty
scuffed and unbuffed
in a two-day shirt
stinking of dog
sweat and sake

the Naked Man
flops across my threshold

begging another poem

~

Dear Reader, I Did Not Swoon

He admires my breasts
my toes, my eyes
the width of my hips
the strength of my thighs

"Strong woman able to bear many children,"
he whispers.

~

Jealousy

The Naked Man's wife
suffers from jealousy
slinking through coffee shops
asking casual questions.
Women turn her away
with soft answers and pity
they know the jealousy flowers
that bloom in her stomach.

Her terrible intuition, sensitive
as litmus, relentless
as a bloodhound, can detect
a single pheromone, the faintest tint
of color in a barely blushing cheek. I remember
the burn of that green venom, etching
like acid through my four-chambered heart—
eating up compassion, ruining contemplation,
diluting care, eroding courage.

That this flirtation so lightly
undertaken might cause such agony
is grounds for terror.

~

Me and Mr. Jones

Remember the Silver Dollar—
skanky little basement dive on a throwaway street
in Grass Valley, CA still coughing up stale tobacco
ten years after the ban; low customers scuttling
down the stairs like cockroaches and a bouncer
so mean even brave men jaywalk to avoid him?

It's different now, all uptown and sleek
sand blasted, dry-walled, scoured, polished
eradicating memories of whiskey and despair.
Spare lines and hardwood floors warmed
by candlelight, cool jazz, timeless barman
wiping down the long bar with a white cloth.
It could be 1920, thirty, forty, or two-thousand-eight
newly opened, not yet discovered,
perfect weeknight setting for a tryst.

We perch at our tiny table
sharing cabernet and gimlets, I gaze
you talk and talk—it all makes sense
reflects my own musing, mingles
with the perfect pitch of a tenor sax.

But I have walked this path before
in other shoes and I see ghosts
pacing the walls, huddled waiting
in the corner of the red leather couch.

Though flame flickers sweetly between us
turning your white shirt cream, dappling
your beautiful neck with gold
though your blue eyes turn navy
dilating with desire, eventually
we must go home again.

And then there's this: fulfillment
nullifies desire, collapses possibilities
concretizes fantasy, defines the dream.

I prefer the swoops and darts of Eros
synchronistic meetings, unplanned rendezvous.
Karma, tossing her gauntlet over a rainbow
time and time again.

~

She Celebrates Her Birthday Eating Ice Cream on the Beach

He moors his boat
in plain sight, positioned
against the setting sun
concealed in its brilliance.

Golden light gilds the woman's
yellow curls, her black dog,
the creamy mound of spumoni
crowning a sugar cone
clutched in her right hand.

The man smells like bay rum.
He fingers his green necktie, red silk shirt
adjusts chocolate-colored corduroy, imagining
her warm tongue, coated with icy cream, licking him
the way she licks that cone.

She stands in surf, toes
buried in sand—water woman
to her core, he can see that.

He loves volatile women of a certain age
but he'll never catch this one.

She flickers in and out
of vision—young, old
fierce, tender, proud, humble.
No doubt she can shapeshift
grow a tail, take to the sea.

He's come too late,
left it too long;
now she belongs completely
to herself.

~

Narcissus

Last night the Naked Man
sat down to calculate trees;
around him stretched a forest
he could not see.

Moonrise limned every leaf
every twig with silver;
brilliant light, bright enough
to read by, drove fox, possum,
deer and hare to shadow
but the Naked Man, entranced, entrained,
transfixed, soaked up illumination.

It filled his lungs, lightened his bones
floated him up past oak and cedar.

Now he bobs outside my window
penis pointing toward the moon
lost in his own reflection.

Golden needles gleam
upon the windowsill.

My fingers twitch
itching to poke and pop
I want to send him whizzing
into that cold glazed lunar face —

a broken nose, red blood dripping
might wake in him, reality.

Instead, I blow a kiss, pull
the shade, leave him to his journey.

Fare well, sweet manchild.
Bon voyage.

~

"I Love Nature"

The Naked Man searches the forest
for clearings open to sky,
i-Tunes trickle through his bones
fingertips beat soft tattoos on plastic keys.

He writes of nature—
odes to moonlit brooks
and thigh-high grass
while, all around him, deer
veer toward other meadows,
porcupine seek different paths,
even earthworms crawl away
to work their fertile magic
elsewhere.

~

His Virtual Harem

The Naked Man stashes
his virtual harem
along the river bank;
taut teenagers break trail,
lush Rubenesque nudes paddle
in the shallows, sleek cougars
stalk the underbrush.

Driven by Demon Loneliness
from cache to cache
he conjures love and lust
from interesting turns of phrase.

Engineering 'accidental' meetings
he eavesdrops behind the wild fig
hoping they will speak of him.

He prefers poets,
loves to a-muse
taunt, titillate, provoke and tease.
If only he could believe
in his own reality
he could enter theirs
but he is the velveteen rabbit;
a Pinocchio whose prick
extends farther with every lie
he tells himself.
~

The Gossip

That Naked Man is a sly one
skulking through the forest
eavesdropping beneath pines
listening for secrets
picking up gossip.

He loves to chase his tales
sniffing out bad-boy stories.

When all else fails
he starts his own rumors
hinting at amours
alleging dubious conquests.

Pretty maidens, beware
his serpent tongue
you never know
where it might have been;
whose secrets it may spill.

~

Doppelganger

The Naked Man hunts shadows
in the forest, chasing down rumors
overturning rocks. Today he found one
hiding in the honeysuckle, pulled it out
and named it *Cynic;* dressed the thing
in torn jeans, shaved its head
and gave it a southern accent.

He's building his shadow a shady cage
in the corner of the parking lot—
makes a nice change from that other one, *Romantic,*
chained to a tie-dyed tent beside the riverside.

Perhaps he'll put his shadows side by side
in a makeshift corral made of boulders and manzanita
let them duke it out with fisticuffs to see who wins.

He doesn't know they're doppelgangers;
twin brothers who would own him.

If the Naked Man wants to break free
he must claim them—call them family
but that's another story.

~

De Nile Is Not Just a River In Egypt

The Naked Man
who swears he hasn't
a mean bone in his body
uses his sex as a weapon
to pierce lush hearts
bleeding them dry
for his own amusement.

~

Wheee...d

The Naked Man
lives off the fat of the land,
the kindness of strangers.
Lush profligate weeds
fill his forest glades.

Green stalks
damp his campfires
smoke and smolder
dim the daylight
but hold the dark
at bay.

He, who refuses darkness
walks a path that turns
and doubles back upon itself,
leading him round and round
the smothering flames
in empty aimless circles.

~

Burnt Bridges

The Naked Man has burned his bridges
no one in town will take him in.
He's forgotten how women network;
friends have friends, who have friends.
He's forgotten how gossip serves
vulnerable members
of the 'weaker' sex.

Now he sleeps
in an unheated canvas womb, flopping
amidst dirty blankets and stained sheets
thumbing a scorecard he keeps
shoved beneath the mattress—
record of conquests
evoking no pleasure
providing no release;
encounters, which no longer
offer proof of love.

~

Eve Comes of Age

His talk fork-splits meaning
into glittering kaleidoscopes
of faceted fragments.

His facile tongue makes you cry
licks tears from your cheeks
moves slowly round your nipples
slides across your tummy
to the secret place below.

He's brilliant like your father,
your brother, ex-lover,
family friend. You've been imprinted;
programmed to surrender.

But though you can't help crying,
or loving
or breaking your heart,

you've learned to deal with serpents
by grabbing them behind the jaw
and slicing off their heads.

~

Lifeline

He makes a list
checks it twice
ready to slouch
into the next poetic milieu
hands in pockets, boyish grin in place
consorting with literary women—
shamans, artists, poets
those whose roots sink deep
into *prima materia*.

Trying not to get his own hands
(or any other part) dirty
he twines round them, catlike
sly, eager; picking up exquisite adjectives
sinuous phrases, robust verbs
hoping their magic
might somehow rub off—
transfer itself without
mud, mess, muck or stink;
toss him a lifeline
he refuses
to throw himself.

~

Stoned and Missing

The Naked Man gathers weed
burns it in green piles
sending smoke signals
to He-Knows-Not-Where.

~

Dark Night

Rain riddles the forest
mist rises, meeting clouds.
The Naked Man
huddles in caves
builds small fires
out of memories.

He squats by the flames
scorching his nuts
freezing his ass
staring into convoluted
tongues of flame
searching for the past.

Blaze falters.
He stirs ashes with fingers
finds an ember
and begins again.

Snot runs from his nose,
dribbles from his chin;
stomach convulses
intestines cramp.

Outside, inch by inch
the fog is lifting.

~

Finish

I'm done with Naked Man
puer aeternus
everlasting youth
Peter Pan
refusing to grow up.

I don't trust him
not to cut off my hand—
which wouldn't
be so bad in itself
if afterwards, he didn't
feed it to the crocodile.

~

Springtime

Today, I caught the Naked Man
dancing a quiet spring jig in the coffee shop
rocking gently on bent knees from foot to foot.
He's thinking of the river's edge where he
can spin, like a whirl-a-gig gone mad,
through stands of oak and pine.

Dew-drenched branches whip winter skin to blush
slough off last night's stale aftermath.
Long arms fling out to rifle manzanita
pull in to clutch pink blossoms to his chest.

Like an ice skater building momentum
he spins, then falls, exhausted,
to mossy ground and sucks
each tiny flower dry

letting bittersweet nectar
trickle drop by drop
down his parched and thirsty throat.

~

Desertion

The Naked Man has moved to another part of the forest
leaving behind an abandoned shrine
and a pile of empty words.
I wish he'd said
good-bye.

~

Acknowledgements

After the Night Before, Intimacy, and *Me and Mr. Jones* previously published in **Sex on Earth** (Six Foot Swells Press, 2008).

Thanks to Julie Valin for her enthusiastic support and a great design of book and cover, and to my daughter, Kathleen Irving for the Naked Man, stepping off the cover into the abyss. Thanks also to Judith Roberts for catching me unaware in her lens.

I also thank the Naked Man, wherever he might be, for his inspiration and love.

***

More about Christine Irving:
writer: http://storycards.wordpress.com
artist: http://adventuresincollage.com/
Priestess: http://christineirving.wordpress.com/

Cover illustration by Kathleen Irving
Cover & Book Design by Julie Valin, The Word Boutique
Author photo by Judith Roberts

6827347R1

Made in the USA
Charleston, SC
13 December 2010